Contents

DAILY LIFE

Read here to learn about what life was like for the children in these stories, and the impact the disaster had at home and school.

NUMBER CRUNCHING

Find out here the details about natural disasters and the damage they cause.

Survivors' lives

Read these boxes to find out what happened to the children in this book when they grew up.

HELPING HAND

Find out how people and organizations have helped to save lives.

On the scene

Read eyewitness accounts of the natural disasters in the survivors' own words.

Some words are printed in bold, **like this**. You can find out what they mean by looking in the glossary on page 30.

Introduction

The soil is so dry and cracked it looks like a jigsaw puzzle. There is not a cloud in the sky. Dust and dirt blow through the air. Crops die. In cities, the water supply falls as rivers and lakes dry up. This is a land suffering from **drought**.

What is a drought?

A drought occurs when an area gets less **moisture** than usual over a period of time. Often a drought is due to a lack of rain. But it can also be caused by too little snow in places that depend on melting snow for moisture.

What is a famine?

A famine is a food shortage that leads to a high number of deaths. A drought can lead to famine, but not in every case. Famines can also be caused by other things besides drought.

Some of the other things that cause famine are plant diseases, bad weather such as floods or hail, and the ruining of soil by people farming it too much. Famine can also happen if food supplies do not reach people because of wars or government failures. Famine is often caused by a combination of one or more of these things.

Surviving Droughts and Famines

Kevin Cunningham

www.raintreepublishers.co.uk
Visit our website to find out
more information about
Raintree books.

To order:
☎ Phone 0845 6044371
🖹 Fax +44 (0) 1865 312263
🖳 Email myorders@raintreepublishers.co.uk

Customers from outside the UK please telephone +44 1865 312262

Raintree is an imprint of **Capstone Global Library Limited**,
a company incorporated in England and Wales having its
registered office at 7 Pilgrim Street, London, EC4V 6LB –
Registered company number: 6695582

Text © Capstone Global Library Limited 2011
First published in hardback in 2011
First published in paperback in 2012
The moral rights of the proprietor have been asserted.

Edited by Louise Galpine and Laura Knowles
Designed by Victoria Allen
Original illustrations © Capstone Global Library Limited 2011
Illustrated by HLSTUDIOS
Picture research by Mica Brancic
Originated by Capstone Global Library Limited
Printed and bound in China by CTPS

ISBN 978 1 406 22217 3 (hardback)
15 14 13 12 11
10 9 8 7 6 5 4 3 2 1

ISBN 978 1 406 22224 1 (paperback)
16 15 14 13 12
10 9 8 7 6 5 4 3 2 1

British Library Cataloguing in Publication Data
Cunningham, Kevin
Surviving droughts and famines. -- (Children's true stories.
Natural disasters).
363.3'4929-dc22
A full catalogue record for this book is available from the
British Library.

Acknowledgements
We would like to thank the following for permission to
reproduce photographs: Alamy p. **24** (© Scott Bowman);
© Corbis p. **13**; Corbis pp. **14** (© Bettmann), **19** (© Peter
Turnley), **23** (© Ashley Cooper), 5 (© FINBARR O'REILLY/
Reuters), **7** (© Michael St. Maur Sheil); FLPA p. **9** (© Nigel
Cattlin); Getty Images pp. **21** (Jo Hale/Stringer), **25** (Torsten
Blackwood/AFP); iStockphoto p. **27** (© Jason Titzer); © Kansas
Historical Society p. **16**; Library of Congress p. **15** (Prints &
Photographs Division, FSA/OWI Collection); Mary Evans pp.
11 (© Illustrated London News Ltd), **8** (© Illustrated London
News Ltd); Panos p. **20** (© Frederic Courbet); Shutterstock
p. **17** (© Shane Wilson Link).

Cover photograph of a child drinking at a tap stand in
Buhona, Ethiopia, reproduced with permission of
Photolibrary/© Caroline Penn.

Quotation on page 8 is from "The Irish Potato Famine,
1847", EyeWitness to History, www.eyewitnesstohistory.com
(2006). Quotation on page 10 is from Thomas Gallagher,
Paddy's Lament, Ireland 1846-1847, Boston: Mariner Books,
1987. Quotation on page 14 is from *Surviving the Dust Bowl*
(transcript: Imogene Glover), PBS, www.pbs.org/wgbh/
americanexperience/features/interview/dustbowl-witness-
glover. Quotation on page 15 is from *Surviving the Dust
Bowl* (transcript: Melt White), PBS, www.pbs.org/wgbh/
americanexperience/features/interview/dustbowl-witness-
white. Quotation on page 16 is from Lee Coleman, "Lucky
to live through it", *Guymon Daily Herald*, March 29, 2010.
Quotation on page 18 is from Mike Woolridge, "Lasting
legacy of Ethiopia's famine", BBC News, 23 October 2009,
news.bbc.co.uk. Quotation on page 21 is from Angela Robson,
"Ethiopian Famine: The Orphans' Stories of Survival",
marieclaire.co.uk. Malcolm Adlington's story on page 23
is from Robert Draper, "Australia's Dry Run", *National
Geographic*, April 2009. Quotation on page 25 is from Phil
Mercer, "New South Wales rains raise hope of end to drought",
BBC News, 9 March 2010, news.bbc.co.uk.

We would like to thank Daniel Block for his invaluable help in
the preparation of this book.

Here, an aid worker is treating a **malnourished** child in the Central African Republic.

DAILY LIFE

Have you ever been so hungry or thirsty you can think about nothing except a drink of water or a mouthful of food? In areas suffering from drought or famine, children live with that feeling every day. Going without enough food or water drains their energy and makes them sick.

Western Ireland: 1845–1849

In 1845 throughout the west of Ireland, something strange happened. One day crops of potatoes seemed fine, but within a couple of weeks they had all turned black and rotted.

The disease that killed them, known as **blight**, had spread everywhere. It seemed as though there was nothing left to eat. Nothing, that is, except the crops belonging to the **landlords**, and they sold those to people in the rest of Britain to make money. In the meantime, the farmers living on their land starved. This became known as the Potato Famine.

This map shows the areas of Ireland that were most affected by potato blight. At the time of the famine, the Republic of Ireland and Northern Ireland was one country.

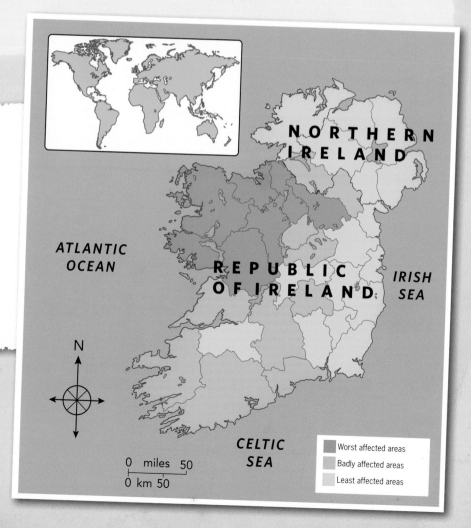

ATLANTIC OCEAN

NORTHERN IRELAND

REPUBLIC OF IRELAND

IRISH SEA

CELTIC SEA

N

0 miles 50
0 km 50

Worst affected areas
Badly affected areas
Least affected areas

Poor government

The British government, which was in control of Ireland at that time, failed to fight the famine successfully. It sent corn to feed the Irish people, but it was **inedible** or cost too much. Then British leaders in government reduced or cut off the supply of corn.

This modern painting of farm workers affected by the potato famine was painted on a wall in Belfast, Northern Ireland, in memory of the disaster.

DAILY LIFE

In the 1840s, Irish **peasants** lived in one-room mud houses and rarely owned land. Instead they worked for landlords who usually lived far away. The peasants gave the crops they grew to the landlord as rent payment.

The peasants' own food came from small gardens. Few crops provided more food on a small patch of land than the potato. Potatoes were also a good source of vitamins and minerals. Because of this, the potato was a very important food, even though the Irish peasants knew it often became diseased.

On the scene

Artist James Mahoney toured Ireland for a British newspaper. He said that while he was in Bridgetown he "saw the dying, the living, and the dead, lying **indiscriminately** upon the same floor, without anything between them and the cold earth, save a few miserable rags upon them".

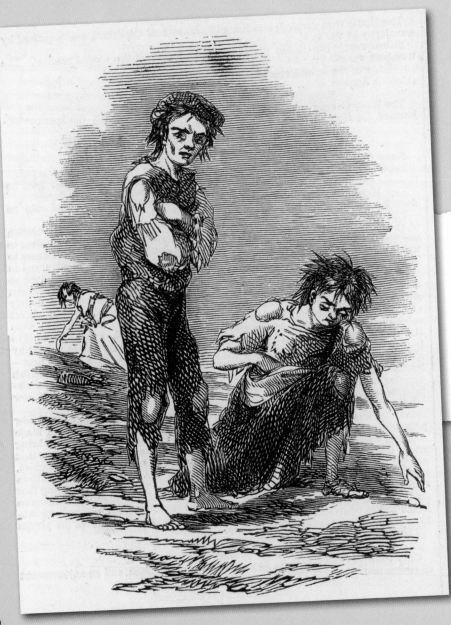

This drawing by eyewitness James Mahoney shows hungry children digging for potatoes.

This potato has been infected by blight. The disease turned potatoes into an inedible mess.

The Running Girl

In the middle of the famine, a hungry young girl, aged about twelve, waited alongside a road. Her family had sold her belongings for food and she had no clothes except for a tattered men's coat. A horse-drawn coach clattered towards her. Inside rode a **minister** named Sidney Godolphin Osborne. Historian Thomas Gallagher told Osborne's story about the girl in his book *Paddy's Lament*.

Desperate

The girl did not just let the coach go by. She began to run alongside it. No matter how fast the horses galloped, she kept up, even though she ran in bare feet. Osborne and his friend were tired of beggars and tried to wave her off. But the girl asked for nothing. She simply ran next to the coach, further and further.

Struggling to survive

Osborne, though annoyed by the girl, could not believe her determination. "On and on she went ever by our side," he said, "using her eyes only to pick her way, never speaking, not even looking at us." His friend, meanwhile, found it harder and harder to refuse her. Finally, after two miles, with the girl bent over from cramps and her feet bleeding, the friend gave her a coin. It was enough to buy a day or two of food for her family.

NUMBER CRUNCHING

Between 1845 and 1855, around two million people decided to leave Ireland for other countries, to find a better future for themselves. This table shows how many went to each country:

Country	Number of people arriving from Ireland between 1845 and 1855
Australia	70,000
Canada	340,000
United Kingdom	300,000
United States	1,500,000

Hunger turns to violence

Desperate people did anything to survive. Mothers begged and farmers ate weeds and nettles. Townspeople battled with soldiers to stop food from being shipped away for sale in Britain.

To deal with this behaviour, new laws were passed in Britain. The laws encouraged landlords to throw families out of their homes in order to clear the unwanted people off their property. Hungry farmers watched as men working for the landlords **tumbled** (knocked down) their houses. Afterwards, the homeless farmers were left to wander or starve in ditches. This caused more people to leave Ireland. Anger against the British government grew.

A landlord tumbled the house of Bridget O'Donnel and her children, shown here.

11

Guymon, Oklahoma, USA: 1933

For 50 years, regular rains helped the wheat grow high on the Great Plains, the mainly flat farmland that stretches from Canada to northern Texas, USA. Then, beginning in 1930, the rain stopped. Endless sunny skies brought record-breaking heat. Crops **withered**. The soil cracked and turned grey.

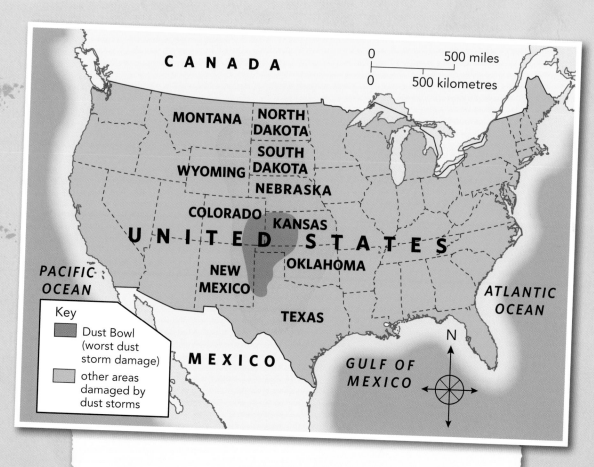

This map shows the area of the United States affected by drought and dust storms in the 1930s. The area shown in dark brown became known as the Dust Bowl.

The Dust Bowl

Due to poor farming practices and too much ploughing, the Great Plains lacked the native plants that once held the soil in place. High winds whipped the dry soil into clouds of dust that blocked out the sunlight, making day seem like night. People struggled to survive each new "**black blizzard**", as they called the dust storms. Even when the wind did not blow, they had to cope with lost crops, and with dust and heat. The worst-hit area became known as the Dust Bowl.

This photograph shows a dust storm coming towards the town of Elkhart, Kansas.

DAILY LIFE

Dust Bowlers fought a constant battle against flying dust. Farmers turned plates upside down to keep them clean and hung wet sheets over cots to keep the dust away from their babies.

Imogene's story

Imogene Davison lived near Guymon, Oklahoma, in the heart of the Dust Bowl. The eight-year-old had survived storms that lasted for hours. While they waited for the dust storms to pass, the Davisons sat in an underground **cellar** where they usually took cover from tornadoes.

"One time I didn't quite get back to the cellar before the dust hit," Imogene later told an American television channel. "The wind and the gravel, it felt like it burned my legs."

Here, a Dust Bowl family battles the wind. The boy on the right, Darrel Coble, grew up to become a farmer in the same region.

Imogene took books into the cellar with her to pass the time. Her father carried tools because dust piled up over the cellar door. When the wind passed, Mr Davison used an axe to break the door, and the handle of a hoe to poke a hole through the dirt to let in air.

Like many people, this family packed up their belongings and moved to another area to get away from the dust storms.

On the scene

On 14 April 1935 – now known as "Black Sunday" – the worst dust storms in American history swept the Great Plains. Melt White was getting ready for church when the storm hit. He said, "I kept bringin' my hand up closer and closer ... and I finally touched the end of my nose and I still couldn't see my hand ... That's how dark it was ..."

Dust everywhere

The scariest dust storm Imogene survived, hit when she was at school. Teachers had to hurry the students from their first-floor classroom to a stairwell downstairs. That was the safest place to be if the wind blew the building down.

Being outside in a storm was far more unpleasant, though. Dust "would just coat the inside of your nose, literally," Imogene told the *Guymon Daily Herald*. "And sometimes your mouth would just get cottony dry because, well, you spit out dirt sometimes … It was pretty awful. But I just thought that was part of living."

Residents of Liberal, Kansas, wore masks as protection against blowing dust.

Dust pneumonia

Those who breathed in too much grit sometimes coughed up dust-clods the size of a pea. In worst cases, dust filled people's lungs. Imogene's younger brother John survived this condition, called **dust pneumonia**. Hundreds of others did not. Many Dust Bowl farmers moved west. The Davisons stayed. By 1940, the rains returned and the Great Plains bloomed again.

Today, the Great Plains of Oklahoma are green again. Farmers use the land to grow crops and feed their animals.

Imogene's life

After high school, Imogene worked on aeroplanes during World War II (1939-1945). She later became a teacher and also spent time as a publisher of a newspaper, earned a Master's degree, and served on Oklahoma's State Board of Education.

Amhara region, Ethiopia: 1984

Between 1981 and 1984, drought killed crops across northern Ethiopia. The government made the problem worse by forcing farmers to move, spending money on wars, and ignoring the hunger. By 1984, famine gripped two areas of the country. The Amhara region in northern Ethiopia was one of the hardest-hit places.

This map shows the Amhara region of Ethiopia. Today, the country still suffers from drought and lack of food.

On the scene

"Fifteen thousand children here now," reported journalist Michael Buerk of the BBC on 23 October 1984. "Suffering. Confused. Lost. Death is all around." Buerk's eyewitness report from a refugee camp in Korem, Ethiopia brought the horrors of starvation to households around the world.

Birtukan's story

Birtukan Abate, born in 1982, lived in a village where people were dying of hunger. One day her parents and two older sisters left to find food. They later died of starvation. Not long after they had gone, a car hit Birtukan. By the time a doctor saw her, her leg was badly infected. Doctors had to **amputate** it to save her life. Every Ethiopian child struggled to survive. Birtukan – left alone and disabled – faced a greater challenge than most.

This Ethiopian woman and her children are starving. They are in a hospital tent in a refugee camp in Sudan, another country in Africa.

Birtukan's journey

An aid worker connected Birtukan to an **orphanage** run by the St Matthew's Children's Fund (SMCF). There, Birtukan received the care she needed. But her childhood wasn't easy. Whilst at the orphanage, Birtukan watched in frustration as families adopted other children. She was always left behind. But the SMCF workers encouraged her to **thrive**. The organization paid for her schooling. Eventually she worked for the education department of the Ethiopian government.

A recent photograph of Birtukan Abate, taken twenty-five years after the famine.

Birtukan told the magazine *Marie Claire*: "the carers at the orphanage taught me to believe in myself … I have a **prosthetic limb**, but I'm alive … It makes me so proud to be able to support myself financially. I could never imagine things would work out so well."

Birhan Woldu became the "face of the famine" when a photographer took her picture as a baby. Birhan survived the disaster and went on to study agricultural science at university.

HELPING HAND

St Matthew's Children's Fund was established to care for orphaned and abandoned children. Today it works with Ethiopian aid groups to continue its work in five Ethiopian regions. The organization also focuses on helping people earn a living so they can provide for themselves.

Forbes, Australia: present day

In parts of southern Australia, there are school-aged children who have never seen a rainstorm. For the past 10 years, the people there have battled the worst drought in the country's recorded history. It is known as the "Big Dry".

Nicole Buttress, a teenager in the small town of Forbes, is old enough to have at least seen a heavy rain. But the Big Dry has drained her town's local lake. When it dried up, Forbes' main tourist attraction was gone.

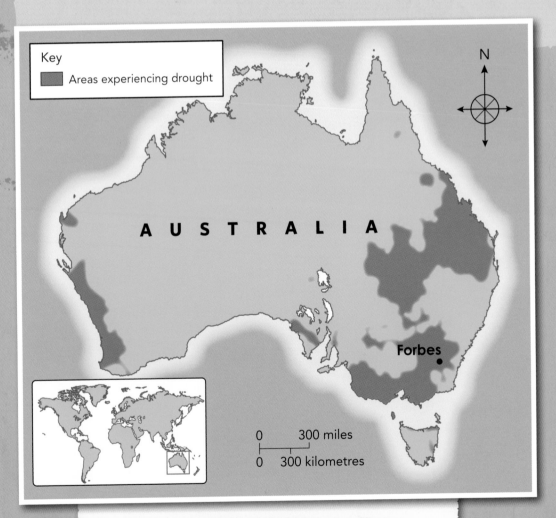

Key

Areas experiencing drought

N

AUSTRALIA

Forbes

0   300 miles

0   300 kilometres

This map shows the areas of Australia affected by drought in recent years.

DAILY LIFE

Malcolm Adlington, a dairy farmer, once owned 500 cows. The drought reduced his herd to 70 animals. Though Adlington continued farming, many local families could not afford to stay. So many people left, in fact, that Adlington's son had to travel 16 kilometres (10 miles) to play with the nearest boy his age.

Hardship and suffering

Farmers in Forbes, like those in the rest of southern Australia, found life difficult. The long stretch of dry weather killed crops and the grass that sheep feed upon. Lost jobs and a lack of money affected the whole town.

The lack of rainfall led to financial hardship for farmers and ranchers. This has been very stressful for them and their families.

Life in the Big Dry

Australians consider drought a part of their lives. But the Big Dry lasted far longer than usual dry spells. It also created new dangers. The soil became so hard that water could not sink into it. When a rare bit of rain fell, it ran off the ground. As it collected in low places such as drainage ditches and dry creek beds, the water created **flash floods**. These flash floods were powerful enough to carry away a car. Dust storms blew into cities. Poisonous snakes searching for moisture slithered into towns and bit adults and children.

People in areas of Australia suffering from drought put out containers to collect all the rainwater they can.

DAILY LIFE

Rules on water use encouraged families to make every drop of water count. Children, for example, showered together to save water. "If it's yellow, let it mellow, if it's brown flush it down" became the new rule for going to the toilet.

On 7 February 2009, a combination of heat, high winds, and drought ignited deadly fires across the state of Victoria, Australia. Here, firefighters are trying to stop the fires from spreading.

On the scene

When rain finally fell on Forbes in early 2010, Nicole Buttress told the BBC "it was like a dream." But it is still uncertain whether the rain has meant the end of the drought or just a break.

Conclusion

Droughts and famines do come to an end eventually. However, it can take a long time. Blight killed the potatoes in Ireland several more times in the 1800s. In Ethiopia, conditions have improved in the last five years, but hunger caused by drought and poverty is a constant threat.

Recovery is possible, however. Rain and smarter farming practices turned the Great Plains of the United States into one of the world's most important food-growing regions, although it is still vulnerable to droughts. Rains in early 2010 also eased Australia's drought, but only time will tell if the Big Dry has ended.

NUMBER CRUNCHING

The World Meteorological Organization has predicted that by the year 2025, between 1 billion and 2.4 billion people will be living in countries where there is a shortage of water. That could be as much as 20 per cent of all the people in the world. The worst affected areas will be in Africa and Asia.

Crops thrive with the right combination of rain, sunlight, and wise farming practices.

Hope for the future?

Today, we grow enough food to feed everyone on Earth. However, due to drought, war, and bad government, the food does not always reach those who need it. Sadly, the world will be coping with drought and famine for years to come.

Mapping drought and famine

Drought or famine can strike anywhere, from the poorest countries to the richest. The map below shows the four events discussed in this book.

NORTH
AMERICA

ATLANTIC
OCEAN

•Guymon

Guymon, Oklahoma

Drought and poor farming practices in the 1930s led to vast dust storms, turning part of the Great Plains into a Dust Bowl.

PACIFIC
OCEAN

SOUTH
AMERICA

Ireland

Around one in every five people either died or left Ireland during the Potato Famine of 1845–1849.

Amhara region, Ethiopia

Over one million people died through famine in Ethiopia during 1984-85. The Amhara region in northern Ethiopia was one of the hardest-hit places.

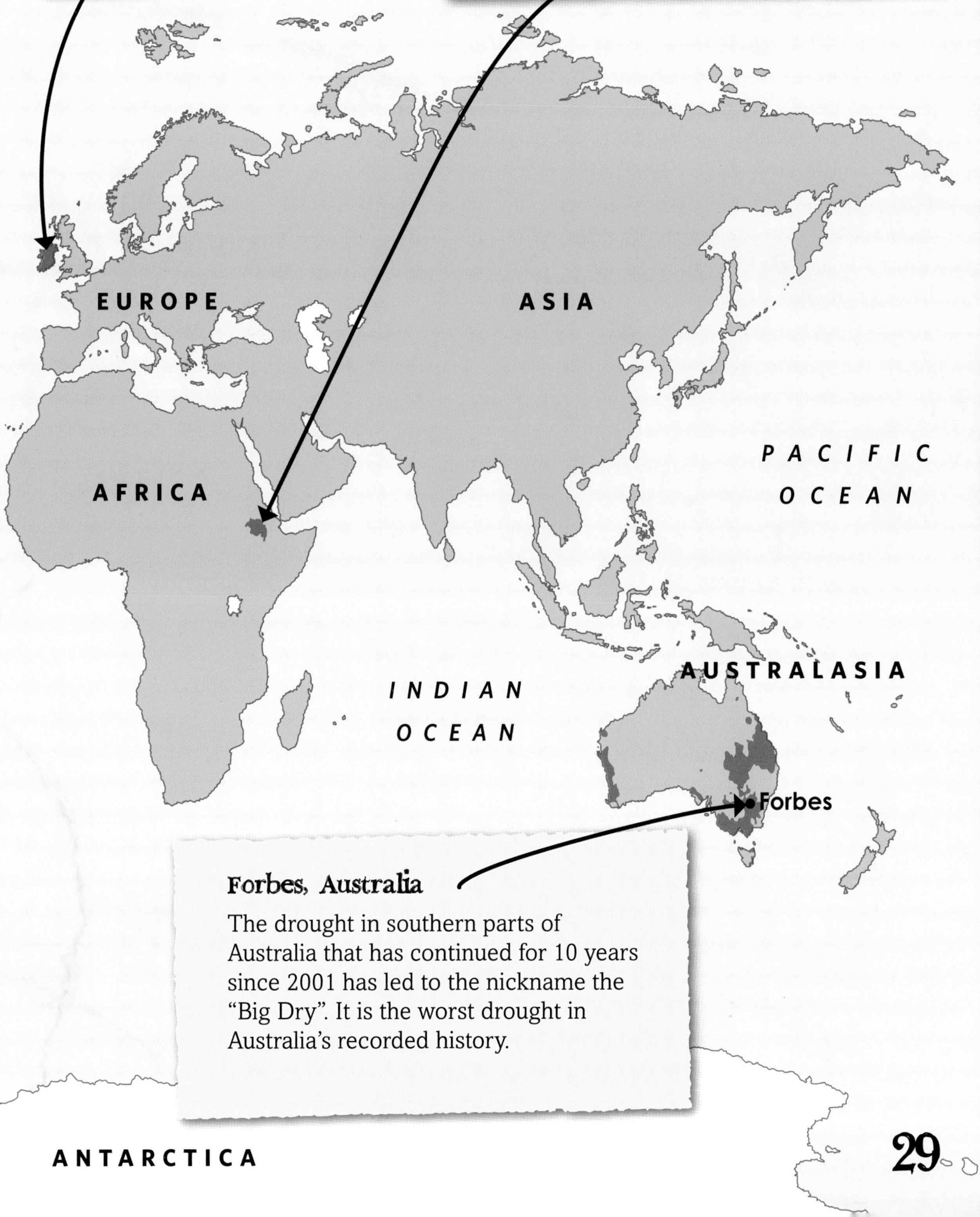

EUROPE

ASIA

AFRICA

PACIFIC OCEAN

INDIAN OCEAN

AUSTRALASIA

Forbes

Forbes, Australia

The drought in southern parts of Australia that has continued for 10 years since 2001 has led to the nickname the "Big Dry". It is the worst drought in Australia's recorded history.

ANTARCTICA

Glossary

amputate in medicine, amputate means to remove or cut off

black blizzard term people used in the 1930s to describe severe dust storms

blight plant disease

cellar underground room used for storage but also as a shelter against violent storms

drought long period with less-than-usual rainfall (or, in some cases, snowfall)

dust pneumonia sometimes deadly condition caused by inhaling too much dirt and dust

flash flood fast-moving flood caused by a sudden rainstorm

indiscriminate done at random or without careful judgement

inedible unfit to eat

landlord property owner who collects money (rent) from people who live or work on his land or in his building

malnourished suffering from a lack of food or not having enough of the right sorts of food

minister person who works for the Christian church, similar to a priest or vicar

moisture water or other liquid

orphanage home for children without parents

peasant farm worker who lives by keeping a small piece of land. In Ireland, peasants also worked for a landlord.

prosthetic limb artificial arm or leg

thrive grow or develop well

tumbled slang word meaning "knocked down"

withered dried up

Find out more

Books

Black Potatoes: The Story of the Great Irish Famine, 1845–1850, Susan Campbell Bartoletti (Houghton Mifflin Harcourt, 2005)

Droughts, Michael Woods and Mary Woods (Lerner, 2006)

The Dust Bowl Through the Lens, Martin W. Sandler (Walker and Company, 2009)

Ethiopia in Pictures, Sam Schultz and Jeffrey Zuehlke (Lerner, 2005)

Years of Dust: The Story of the Dust Bowl, Albert Marrin (Dutton, 2009)

On the Web

www.pbs.org/wgbh/americanexperience/films/dustbowl
This film tells the story of the farmers who went to farm on the Southern Plains of Texas, Oklahoma, and Kansas, but who had to survive 10 years of drought.

www.bbc.co.uk/radio4/womanshour/2005_28_fri_01.shtml
Visit this web page to listen to a BBC interview with Birhan Woldu, aged three during the famine of Ethiopia, and now an adult, sharing her experiences.

www.bbc.co.uk/history/british/victorians/famine_01.shtml
This BBC web page has lots of information about the Irish Potato Famine.

www.weru.ksu.edu/new_weru/multimedia/dustbowl/dustbowlpics.html
You can look at Kansas State University's photographs of the Dust Bowl here.

http://ngm.nationalgeographic.com/2009/04/murray-darling/toensing-photography
This is the National Geographic's photo gallery on the Australian Drought.

A place to visit

Famine Memorial
Custom House Quay, Docklands
Dublin, Ireland

Index